THE WEALTH CREATION HANDBOOK:
UNLOCKING FINANCIAL SUCCESS

JOHN KENNEDY AKOTIA

Copyright © 2023 JOHN KENNEDY AKOTIA

All rights reserved. No part of this publication may be used or reproduced in any form or by any means, or stored in a database or retrieval system, or transmitted in any form or by any means without prior written permission, except in the case of brief quotations embodied in critical articles and reviews.

Request for information should be addressed to
John Kennedy Akotia
Destiny Impact Publications
P. O. BG 106
Bolgatanga, UER, Ghana, W/A

Mobile 1: +233-24 445 1746
Mobile 2: +233-20 622 9855
E-mail: akotiakennedy@gmail.com

TABLE OF CONTENTS

INTRODUCTION TO WEALTH CREATION 4
BUILDING A WEALTH MINDSET 7
SETTING FINANCIAL GOALS 11
MANAGING PERSONAL FINANCES 15
INVESTING FOR WEALTH CREATION 21
ENTREPRENEURSHIP AND BUSINESS VENTURES 28
REAL ESTATE INVESTMENTS 35
STOCK MARKET AND TRADING 42
BUILDING MULTIPLE STREAMS OF INCOME 49
WEALTH PRESERVATION AND LEGACY PLANNING....55
MASTERING THE PSYCHOLOGY OF WEALTH 61
CREATING A WEALTHY FUTURE 67
CONCLUSION 73
APPENDIX: ADDITIONAL RESOURCES 76

CHAPTER ONE

INTRODUCTION TO WEALTH CREATION

1.1 Defining Wealth

Wealth can be defined as the accumulation of valuable assets, resources, and abundance in various aspects of life, including financial, intellectual, emotional, and spiritual. It goes beyond the mere possession of money and encompasses the ability to create opportunities, experience freedom, and make a positive impact on oneself and others.

1.2 The Importance of Wealth Creation

Wealth creation is essential for individuals and societies to thrive and progress. It provides the means to meet our needs, pursue our dreams, and enjoy a comfortable lifestyle. Additionally, wealth creation allows us to contribute to our communities, support charitable causes, and create a lasting legacy.

1.3 Understanding Financial Success

Financial success is a significant component of wealth creation, but it is not limited to monetary achievements alone. It encompasses achieving financial independence, having a stable income, managing debt effectively, and making wise investment decisions. Financial success also involves aligning our financial goals with our values, living within our means, and finding a balance between short-term gratification and long-term wealth creation.

In this book, "**The Wealth Creation Handbook: Unlocking Financial Success,**" we will explore the principles, strategies, and mindset necessary to embark on a journey of wealth creation. Whether you are starting from scratch or seeking to enhance your existing financial situation, this book will provide you with practical guidance and insights to make informed decisions, overcome challenges, and unlock your full potential for financial success.

We will delve into various areas of wealth creation, including building a wealth mindset, setting financial goals, managing personal finances, investing, entrepreneurship, real estate, stock market trading, multiple streams of income, wealth preservation, and the psychology of wealth. Each chapter will equip you with the knowledge and tools to navigate the complexities of wealth creation and develop a comprehensive approach that aligns with your unique circumstances and aspirations.

It is important to note that wealth creation is not a one-size-fits-all endeavour. Each individual's path to financial success may differ based on their goals, risk tolerance, and personal preferences. This book will provide you with a broad range of strategies and insights, allowing you to tailor your wealth creation journey to suit your specific needs and aspirations.

By adopting the principles and strategies outlined in this book and taking consistent action, you can unlock the doors to financial success, create wealth, and enjoy the benefits that come with it. Remember, wealth creation is a lifelong journey, and the process itself can be as rewarding as the destination. So, let us embark on this transformative journey together and unlock the doors to financial abundance and fulfilment.

CHAPTER TWO

BUILDING A WEALTH MINDSET

2.1 Developing a Positive Relationship with Money

To embark on the path of wealth creation, it is crucial to develop a positive relationship with money. Many people harbour deep-rooted beliefs and emotions around money that can either support or hinder their financial success. In this section, we will explore strategies to cultivate a healthy money mindset, including:

Recognizing and challenging limiting beliefs:
Identify any negative beliefs or attitudes you may have about money and challenge them. Replace scarcity thinking with an abundance mindset that embraces the idea of unlimited possibilities.

Practicing gratitude:
Cultivate a sense of gratitude for the money you have and the opportunities it brings. Focus on the abundance in your life rather than dwelling on scarcity or lack.

Embracing money as a tool for growth:

View money as a resource that can help you achieve your goals, make a positive impact, and create opportunities for yourself and others. Shift from a mindset of money as a source of stress to one of empowerment and abundance.

2.2 Overcoming Limiting Beliefs

Limiting beliefs are deeply ingrained thoughts or assumptions that hold us back from reaching our full potential. In the context of wealth creation, they can manifest as beliefs such as "money is evil" or "wealth is only for a select few." Overcoming these beliefs is essential for building a wealth mindset. Here are some strategies to help you overcome limiting beliefs:

Awareness and reflection:
Start by becoming aware of your limiting beliefs around money. Reflect on where these beliefs originated and how they have influenced your financial decisions and actions.

Challenging and reframing beliefs:
Once you have identified your limiting beliefs, challenge them by examining the evidence that supports or contradicts them. Replace negative beliefs with positive affirmations that align with your wealth creation goals.

Surrounding yourself with positive influences:
Surround yourself with individuals who have a positive mindset towards money and success. Seek out mentors, role models, or supportive communities that can reinforce your new beliefs and inspire you on your wealth creation journey.

2.3 Cultivating a Wealthy Mindset

Building a wealthy mindset involves adopting the attitudes, habits, and behaviours that support wealth creation. Here are some key elements of a wealthy mindset:

Growth mindset:
Embrace a mindset of continuous learning and personal growth. See challenges as opportunities for growth and view failures as valuable lessons that propel you forward.

Taking calculated risks:
Be willing to step outside your comfort zone and take calculated risks. Understand that wealth creation often requires venturing into new territories and embracing uncertainty.

Persistence and resilience:
Cultivate the ability to persist in the face of setbacks and challenges. Develop resilience by

bouncing back from failures, learning from mistakes, and maintaining a positive attitude.

Goal-oriented mindset:
Set clear, specific, and meaningful financial goals. Break them down into actionable steps and regularly review and adjust them as necessary.

Embracing abundance and generosity:
Embrace the belief that there is enough wealth and success to go around. Practice generosity by giving back to others and sharing your wealth in meaningful ways.

Developing a wealth mindset is a continuous process that requires self-awareness, reflection, and consistent practice. By consciously adopting these strategies and nurturing a positive mindset, you will create a solid foundation for your wealth creation journey and open yourself up to the abundance that awaits you. Remember, building a wealth mindset is as important as acquiring financial knowledge and taking action, as it sets the stage for sustainable and fulfilling wealth creation.

CHAPTER THREE

SETTING FINANCIAL GOALS

3.1 The Power of Goal Setting

Setting clear and specific financial goals is a crucial step in the wealth creation journey. Goals provide direction, motivation, and a roadmap for achieving financial success. In this chapter, we will explore the power of goal setting and provide a step-by-step guide to setting meaningful financial goals.

3.2 Aligning Goals with Values and Aspirations

Before diving into goal setting, it is important to align your financial goals with your values and aspirations. Take the time to reflect on what truly matters to you and what you want to achieve in your life. Consider your long-term vision, your passions, and the legacy you want to leave behind. By aligning your goals with your core values, you will create a strong foundation for sustainable wealth creation.

3.3 Types of Financial Goals

Financial goals can be categorized into short-term, medium-term, and long-term goals. Short-term goals typically span one year or less and may include things like paying off a credit card debt or saving for a vacation. Medium-term goals span one to five years and may include saving for a down payment on a house or starting a business. Long-term goals are typically more than five years and may include goals such as achieving financial independence or building a retirement fund.

3.4 SMART Goal Setting

To make your financial goals more effective and achievable, it is helpful to follow the SMART goal-setting framework:

Specific: Clearly define your financial goal. Avoid vague statements and be specific about what you want to accomplish. For example, instead of saying "I want to save money," specify the amount you want to save and by when.

Measurable: Establish metrics to track your progress and measure the success of your goals. Set benchmarks or milestones along the way to ensure you are making tangible progress.

Attainable: Ensure that your goals are realistic and attainable within your current financial situation. Consider your income, expenses, and other financial commitments when setting your goals. While it is important to aim high, setting unrealistic goals can lead to frustration and disappointment.

Relevant: Your goals should align with your overall financial vision and aspirations. Ensure that they are relevant to your values, priorities, and long-term objectives. Your goals should have a meaningful impact on your financial well-being and contribute to your overall wealth creation journey.

Time-bound: Set a deadline for achieving your financial goals. Having a specific timeframe creates a sense of urgency and helps you stay focused and accountable. Break down your goals into smaller time-bound targets to make them more manageable and trackable.

3.5 Creating an Action Plan

Once you have set your financial goals, it is essential to create an action plan to turn them into a reality. Break down your goals into smaller actionable steps and prioritize them based on their importance and urgency. Consider what resources, skills, and support you may need to accomplish each step. Regularly review and adjust your action plan as needed to stay on track and adapt to changing circumstances.

3.6 Tracking Progress and Celebrating Milestones

Tracking your progress is crucial for staying motivated and accountable. Regularly review your goals and monitor your progress against the benchmarks or milestones you have set. Celebrate your achievements along the way, whether it's reaching a savings target or paying off a debt. Recognizing and celebrating milestones will reinforce your commitment to your financial goals and provide a sense of accomplishment.

Setting financial goals is a powerful tool for wealth creation. By aligning your goals with your values, using the SMART framework, creating an action plan, and tracking your progress, you will be on your way to achieving financial success. Remember, goals provide the roadmap, but it is your consistent effort, determination, and perseverance that will ultimately lead you to your desired financial destination.

CHAPTER 4

MANAGING PERSONAL FINANCES

4.1 The Importance of Financial Management

Effective financial management is a cornerstone of wealth creation. It involves developing habits and strategies to track, organize, and optimize your personal finances. In this chapter, we will explore key principles and practices for managing your personal finances.

4.2 Budgeting and Cash Flow Management

Budgeting is a fundamental tool for managing personal finances. It helps you allocate your income effectively, track your expenses, and ensure that you are living within your means. In this section, we will discuss the following aspects of budgeting:

Creating a budget:
Learn how to create a comprehensive budget that takes into account your income, fixed expenses, variable expenses, savings goals, and debt obligations.

Tracking expenses:
Discover methods for tracking your expenses, such as using spreadsheets, budgeting apps, or financial management software. Regularly reviewing and categorizing your expenses will provide insights into your spending habits and areas where you can make adjustments.

Identifying areas for improvement:
Analyse your budget to identify areas where you can reduce expenses or reallocate funds to align with your financial goals. This may involve cutting unnecessary expenses, renegotiating bills, or finding more cost-effective alternatives.

4.3 Debt Management

Managing debt is a critical component of personal finance. It is essential to develop strategies for handling debt responsibly and minimizing its impact on your financial well-being. This section will cover the following topics:

Debt assessment:
Evaluate your existing debt and understand its terms, interest rates, and repayment schedules. Categorize your debts based on their priority and urgency for repayment.

Debt reduction strategies:

Explore various strategies for paying off debt, such as the snowball method (paying off smaller debts first) or the avalanche method (paying off debts with the highest interest rates first). Consider consolidation options or negotiating with creditors to lower interest rates or payment terms.

Avoiding new debt:
Develop strategies to avoid accumulating new debt. This may involve creating an emergency fund, practicing mindful spending or frugal living, and distinguishing between wants and needs.

4.4 Building an Emergency Fund

Having an emergency fund is crucial for financial stability. It provides a safety net in case of unexpected expenses or income disruptions. In this section, we will discuss:

Determining the appropriate emergency fund size:
Consider factors such as your monthly expenses, income stability, and risk tolerance when determining the size of your emergency fund.

Saving for emergencies:
Learn strategies for saving money specifically for emergencies, such as setting up automatic

transfers to a separate account or using a portion of your income specifically designated for emergencies.

Managing emergency expenses:
Develop a plan for handling unexpected expenses without derailing your overall financial goals. This may involve prioritizing expenses, negotiating payment terms, or seeking assistance when necessary.

4.5 Saving and Investing

Saving and investing are key components of wealth creation. This section will cover the following aspects:

Setting savings goals:
Determine your short-term and long-term savings goals, such as saving for a down payment on a house, retirement, or education expenses.

Choosing appropriate savings vehicles:
Explore different savings options, such as high-yield savings accounts, certificates of deposit (CDs), or money market accounts. Consider factors such as liquidity, interest rates, and risk tolerance when selecting savings vehicles.

Introduction to investing:

Gain a basic understanding of investment options, including stocks, bonds, mutual funds, and real estate. Consider working with a financial advisor or doing thorough research before making investment decisions.

Risk management:
Understand the concept of risk and develop strategies for managing and mitigating investment risks. Diversification, asset allocation, and periodic portfolio reviews are essential components of risk management.

4.6 Regular Financial Check-ups and Reviews

Regularly reviewing and assessing your personal finances is crucial for maintaining financial health. This section will guide you on how to conduct financial check-ups and reviews:

Frequency of reviews:
Determine how frequently you should review your financial situation. It may vary based on personal circumstances, but aim for at least an annual review.

Assessing progress:
Evaluate your progress towards your financial goals, identify areas that require improvement,

and make necessary adjustments to your financial plan.

Seeking professional guidance:
Consider consulting with a financial advisor or planner to gain expert insight and guidance on managing your personal finances effectively.

Effective management of personal finances is essential for building wealth and achieving financial success. By implementing budgeting strategies, managing debt responsibly, building an emergency fund, saving, investing, and conducting regular financial reviews, you will be well-equipped to make informed decisions and navigate your financial journey with confidence.
Remember, financial management is a lifelong process, so continue to educate yourself, adapt to changing circumstances, and remain proactive in your approach to personal finance.

CHAPTER FIVE

INVESTING FOR WEALTH CREATION

5.1 The Importance of Investing

Investing is a powerful tool for wealth creation. It involves allocating your money into various assets or financial instruments with the aim of generating returns and growing your wealth over time. In this chapter, we will explore the fundamentals of investing and how it can contribute to your overall wealth creation goals.

5.2 Understanding Risk and Return

Investing inherently involves risk, and understanding the relationship between risk and return is crucial. Higher potential returns typically come with higher levels of risk. In this section, we will discuss:

- **Risk tolerance:**

Assess your risk tolerance, which is your comfort level with taking on investment risks. Consider factors such as your financial goals, time horizon, and personal circumstances when determining your risk tolerance.

- **Diversification:**

Learn about the importance of diversifying your investment portfolio. Diversification helps spread risk by investing in a variety of assets across different industries, regions, and asset classes.

- **Asset allocation:**

Understand the concept of asset allocation, which involves deciding how to distribute your investment capital among different asset classes, such as stocks, bonds, real estate, and cash. Asset allocation should align with your risk tolerance, financial goals, and time horizon.

5.3 Types of Investments

There are various types of investments available, each with its own characteristics, risk profiles, and potential returns. In this section, we will explore some common investment options, including:

Stocks:

Learn about investing in individual stocks, which represent ownership shares in publicly traded companies. Understand the factors that influence stock prices and the importance of conducting thorough research before making investment decisions.

Bonds:

Explore the world of fixed-income investments, such as government bonds, corporate bonds, and municipal bonds. Understand how bonds work, their risk profiles, and how they generate returns through interest payments.

Mutual Funds and Exchange-Traded Funds (ETFs):
Discover the benefits of investing in mutual funds and ETFs, which pool money from multiple investors to invest in a diversified portfolio of stocks, bonds, or other assets. Learn about the different types of funds, their costs, and how they are managed.

Real Estate:
Gain insights into real estate investing, including rental properties, commercial properties, and real estate investment trusts (REITs). Understand the potential risks and rewards associated with investing in real estate and the importance of thorough market research.

5.4 Investment Strategies

Developing an investment strategy is crucial for successful wealth creation. In this section, we will discuss different investment strategies, including:

Long-term investing:

Understand the benefits of a long-term investment approach, where you hold investments for an extended period, allowing them to potentially grow and compound over time.

Dollar-cost averaging:
Learn about the concept of dollar-cost averaging, which involves investing a fixed amount of money at regular intervals, regardless of market conditions. This strategy can help mitigate the impact of market volatility and potentially lead to favourable average purchase prices.

Value investing:
Explore the principles of value investing, which involves identifying undervalued stocks or assets and investing in them with the expectation of long-term growth. Understand the importance of fundamental analysis and identifying intrinsic value.

Growth investing:
Discover the principles of growth investing, which focuses on investing in companies with strong growth potential. Learn about identifying growth trends, analysing financial statements, and assessing a company's competitive advantage.

5.5 Risk Management and Portfolio Diversification

Managing risk and maintaining a diversified investment portfolio are essential for long-term success when it comes to wealth creation. In this section, we will cover risk management strategies and portfolio diversification:

Risk management strategies:
Learn about risk management techniques, such as setting stop-loss orders, using trailing stops, and employing hedging strategies to protect your investments from significant losses.

Portfolio diversification:
Understand the importance of diversifying your investment portfolio by spreading your investments across different asset classes, sectors, and regions. Diversification can help reduce the impact of individual investment performance on your overall portfolio.

5.6 Monitoring and Reviewing Your Investments

Regularly monitoring and reviewing your investments is critical for ensuring that they align with your financial goals and adjusting your strategy when necessary. This section will cover the following three strategies:

Investment performance tracking:
Learn how to track and analyse the performance of your investments using various metrics and tools. Regularly review your investments to evaluate their performance and make informed decisions.

Rebalancing:
Understand the concept of portfolio rebalancing, which involves adjusting your asset allocation to maintain desired risk levels and optimize returns. Learn when and how to rebalance your portfolio.

Seeking professional advice:
Consider working with a financial advisor or investment professional to gain expert guidance, especially if you are new to investing or have complex financial needs.

Investing for wealth creation requires knowledge, strategy, and a long-term perspective. By understanding risk and return, exploring different investment options, developing an investment strategy, managing risk through diversification, and regularly monitoring and reviewing your investments, you can position yourself for long-term financial success.

Remember, investing involves inherent risks, so ensure you conduct thorough research, stay informed, and make informed investment decisions that align with your financial goals and risk tolerance.

CHAPTER SIX

ENTREPRENEURSHIP AND BUSINESS VENTURES

6.1 The Entrepreneurial Mindset

Entrepreneurship is a pathway to wealth creation that involves identifying opportunities, taking calculated risks, and creating value through innovative business ventures. In this chapter, we will explore the entrepreneurial mindset and the steps involved in starting and growing a successful business.

6.2 Identifying Business Opportunities

Successful entrepreneurs are adept at identifying and capitalizing on business opportunities. This section will guide you on how to recognize potential business ideas and evaluate their feasibility, including:

Market research:
Conduct thorough market research to identify gaps, trends, and consumer needs. Understand your target market, competition, and potential demand for your products or services.

Problem-solving:
Look for problems or pain points in the market that you can address with your business idea. Identify ways to provide value and solve customer challenges more effectively than existing solutions.

Innovation and differentiation:
Seek opportunities to innovate and differentiate your business from competitors. Identify unique selling points and value propositions that set your business apart in the market.

6.3 Developing a Business Plan

A well-crafted business plan serves as a roadmap for your entrepreneurial journey. In this section, we will discuss the key components of a business plan, including:

Executive summary:
Provide a concise overview of your business idea, mission, and vision.

Market analysis:
Present a detailed analysis of your target market, including its size, demographics, trends, and competition.

Product or service description:

Describe your products or services, their features, benefits, and unique selling points.

Marketing and sales strategies:
Outline your marketing and sales approaches, including your target audience, pricing strategy, promotional activities, and distribution channels.

Operational plan:
Detail your business operations, including the location, equipment, supply chain, and production processes.

Financial projections:
Present your financial forecasts, including revenue projections, expenses, profitability analysis, and funding requirements.

6.4 Securing Funding

Securing adequate funding is often a critical factor in launching and growing a successful business. This section will cover various funding options for entrepreneurs, including:

Self-funding:
Use personal savings, investments, or assets to finance your business. This may include bootstrapping, where you start small and grow organically.

Debt financing:
Explore options such as bank loans, lines of credit, or microloans to obtain capital for your business. Understand the terms, interest rates, and repayment obligations associated with different types of debt financing.

Equity financing:
Consider seeking investors who provide capital in exchange for equity or ownership in your business. This may include angel investors, venture capitalists, or crowd funding platforms.

Grants and subsidies:
Research grants, subsidies, and government programs that provide financial support to start-ups and small businesses. These can be valuable sources of non-dilutive funding.

6.5 Building a Strong Team

Entrepreneurship often requires assembling a capable and dedicated team to support your business. In this section, we will discuss strategies for building a strong team, including:

Defining roles and responsibilities:
Clearly define the roles and responsibilities of each team member to ensure clarity and alignment.

Hiring and recruitment:
Develop effective hiring and recruitment processes to attract and select the right talent for your business. Consider skills, experience, cultural fit, and shared values when making hiring decisions.

Leadership and management:
Cultivate strong leadership skills and create a positive work culture that fosters collaboration, innovation, and employee growth.

Training and development:
Invest in training and development programs to enhance the skills and capabilities of your team members. This will contribute to their professional growth and the overall success of your business.

6.6 Scaling and Growth Strategies

Once your business is established, scaling and growth become key objectives. This section will cover strategies for scaling your business and achieving sustainable growth, including:

Operational efficiency:
Streamline your business operations and processes to improve productivity, reduce costs, and enhance overall efficiency.

Market expansion:
Explore new markets, target new customer segments, or introduce new products or services to expand your reach and revenue potential.

Strategic partnerships:
Identify opportunities for strategic partnerships, collaborations, or alliances that can help accelerate your business growth. This may involve joint ventures, distribution agreements, or strategic acquisitions.

Innovation and adaptation:
Continuously innovate and adapt to changing market dynamics and customer preferences. Stay abreast of industry trends, technology advancements, and evolving consumer needs.

Entrepreneurship offers the potential for significant wealth creation. By embracing the entrepreneurial mindset, identifying business opportunities, developing a comprehensive business plan, securing funding, building a strong team, and implementing effective scaling and growth strategies, you can increase your chances of building a successful and profitable business venture.

Remember, entrepreneurship requires perseverance, resilience, and continuous learning.

Stay focused on your goals, seek mentorship and guidance when needed, and adapt to the ever-changing business landscape to drive long-term success.

CHAPTER SEVEN

REAL ESTATE INVESTMENTS

7.1 Introduction to Real Estate Investments

Real estate investments can be a powerful wealth-building strategy due to their potential for appreciation, rental income, and tax benefits. In this chapter, we will explore the basics of real estate investing and how to navigate this lucrative asset class.

7.2 Types of Real Estate Investments

There are various types of real estate investments to consider, each with its own characteristics and potential returns. This section will cover:

Residential properties:
Explore investing in single-family homes, multi-family properties, condominiums, or vacation rentals. Understand the market dynamics, rental demand, and potential rental income for residential properties.

Commercial properties:

Discover opportunities in commercial real estate, such as office buildings, retail spaces, industrial properties, and warehouses. Learn about lease terms, tenant quality, and market trends affecting commercial properties.

Real Estate Investment Trusts (REITs):
Understand the concept of REITs, which allow investors to pool their money to invest in a diversified portfolio of real estate assets. Learn about the different types of REITs, their performance, and how to invest in them.

Real Estate Crowd funding:
Explore the world of real estate crowd funding platforms that allow individuals to invest in specific real estate projects or properties. Understand the risks, potential returns, and due diligence involved in real estate crowd funding.

7.3 Evaluating Real Estate Investments

When considering a real estate investment, thorough evaluation is essential. This section will discuss key factors to consider when evaluating real estate opportunities, including:

Location analysis:
Assess the location of the property, including factors such as neighbourhood quality, proximity

to amenities, schools, transportation, and potential for future development or growth.

Property condition and potential:
Evaluate the condition of the property and its potential for value appreciation or renovation. Consider factors such as property age, maintenance requirements, and potential renovation or improvement opportunities.

Cash flow analysis:
Analyse the potential rental income and expenses associated with the property. Consider factors such as rental rates, vacancy rates, property management costs, maintenance expenses, and property taxes.

Financing options:
Explore different financing options, such as mortgages, to determine the affordability and feasibility of the investment. Consider interest rates, loan terms, down payment requirements, and potential cash flow implications.

Market trends and projections:
Stay informed about local and national real estate market trends, supply and demand dynamics, and economic indicators that can impact property values and rental markets.

7.4 Risk Management in Real Estate Investments

Real estate investments come with their share of risks, and understanding and managing these risks is crucial. This section will cover:

Market risk:
Recognize that real estate markets can experience fluctuations and downturns. Understand the cyclical nature of real estate and develop strategies to mitigate market risks.

Financing risk:
Be aware of the risks associated with borrowing money for real estate investments. Assess your ability to meet mortgage payments, anticipate interest rate changes, and evaluate potential cash flow challenges.

Property-specific risks:
Evaluate property-specific risks, such as property damage, legal issues, tenant turnover, or regulatory changes. Develop contingency plans and insurance strategies to mitigate these risks.

Portfolio diversification:
Consider diversifying your real estate investments across different property types, locations, and risk

profiles. This can help spread risk and enhance overall portfolio stability.

7.5 Property Management and Maintenance

Proper property management and maintenance are crucial for the success of real estate investments. This section will cover:

Property management options:
Decide whether to manage the property yourself or hire a professional property management company. Understand the responsibilities involved, such as tenant screening, rent collection, property maintenance, and legal compliance.

Maintenance and repairs:
Develop a proactive maintenance plan to preserve the condition and value of your property. Regularly assess and address maintenance needs, and budget for repairs and renovations as necessary.

Tenant management:
If renting out the property, establish effective tenant management processes. Develop tenant selection criteria, establish clear lease agreements, and promptly address tenant concerns and issues.

7.6 Tax Considerations in Real Estate Investments

Real estate investments offer several tax advantages that can contribute to your wealth creation. This section will discuss:

Tax deductions:
Understand the tax deductions available for real estate investments, such as mortgage interest, property taxes, depreciation, and expenses related to property management and maintenance.

1031 exchanges:
Explore the concept of 1031 exchanges, which allow you to defer capital gain taxes when selling one investment property and acquiring another like-kind property.

Tax implications of rental income:
Familiarize yourself with the tax implications of rental income, including reporting requirements, deductible expenses, and potential tax brackets.

Real estate investments can be a profitable avenue for wealth creation. By understanding the different types of real estate investments, evaluating opportunities diligently, managing risks effectively, maintaining properties, and optimizing tax advantages, you can maximize the potential returns from your real estate investments.

Remember to stay informed about market trends, seek professional advice when needed, and continuously monitor and adapt your investment strategy to align with your financial goals.

CHAPTER EIGHT

STOCK MARKET AND TRADING

8.1 Introduction to the Stock Market

The stock market provides opportunities for wealth creation through buying and selling stocks of publicly traded companies. In this chapter, we will explore the fundamentals of the stock market, understanding stocks, and the various aspects of stock trading.

8.2 Understanding Stocks

Before diving into stock trading, it is important to understand the basics of stocks. This section will cover:

What is a stock?
Learn what stocks represent, which are shares of ownership in a company. Understand the rights and privileges that come with stock ownership, such as voting rights and dividends.

Types of stocks:
Explore different types of stocks, including common stocks and preferred stocks. Understand

the differences between these types of stocks in terms of ownership rights and potential returns.

Stock valuation:
Learn about the factors that influence stock prices, including company performance, industry trends, market conditions, and investor sentiment. Understand fundamental analysis and technical analysis as methods for evaluating stock values.

8.3 Investing in Stocks

Investing in stocks can be a long-term strategy for wealth creation. This section will cover key considerations for stock investing, including:

Setting investment goals:
Define your investment goals, such as capital appreciation, dividend income, or a combination of both. Determine your risk tolerance and time horizon to guide your investment decisions.

Research and analysis:
Conduct thorough research and analysis on companies before investing in their stocks. Evaluate financial statements, company performance, industry trends, competitive advantage, and management quality.

Building a diversified portfolio:
Understand the importance of diversification by investing in a variety of stocks across different industries, sectors, and market capitalizations. Diversification helps spread risk and potentially enhance returns.

Long-term investing:
Embrace a long-term investment approach and avoid short-term market fluctuations. Understand the power of compounding and the benefits of staying invested in quality companies for the long haul.

8.4 Stock Trading Strategies

Stock trading involves buying and selling stocks with the aim of making short-term profits. This section will discuss various stock trading strategies, including:

Day trading:
Explore the concept of day trading, where traders buy and sell stocks within the same trading day. Understand the risks and challenges associated with day trading, including market volatility and the need for quick decision-making.

Swing trading:

Learn about swing trading, which involves holding stocks for a few days to a few weeks to capture short-term price movements. Understand technical analysis tools and chart patterns used in swing trading.

Value investing:
Discover the principles of value investing, which involve identifying undervalued stocks and holding them for the long term. Understand the importance of fundamental analysis and assessing a company's intrinsic value.

Growth investing:
Explore growth investing, which focuses on investing in companies with high growth potential. Learn about identifying growth trends, analysing financial statements, and assessing a company's competitive advantage.

8.5 Risk Management in Stock Trading

Managing risk is crucial when engaging in stock trading. This section will cover risk management strategies, including:

Setting stop-loss orders:
Understand the concept of stop-loss orders, which automatically sell a stock when it reaches a

predetermined price. Stop-loss orders help limit potential losses and protect capital.

Portfolio diversification:
Diversify your stock trading portfolio by spreading your investments across different stocks and sectors. Diversification helps mitigate the impact of individual stock performance on your overall portfolio.

Risk-reward assessment:
Evaluate the risk-reward ratio of each trade before entering a position. Set realistic profit targets and consider the potential downside risk when making trading decisions.

Continuous learning and research:
Stay informed about market trends, company news, and industry developments. Continuously update your knowledge and refine your trading strategies through ongoing learning and research.

8.6 Trading Tools and Resources

Leveraging the right tools and resources can enhance your stock trading experience. This section will discuss:

Online brokerage platforms:

Explore online brokerage platforms that provide access to stock markets and trading tools. Compare features, fees, and user experiences to choose a platform that suits your trading needs.

Technical analysis tools:
Learn about popular technical analysis tools, such as moving averages, oscillators, and chart patterns. These tools can help identify trends, entry points, and exit signals in stock trading.

Fundamental analysis resources:
Discover resources for conducting fundamental analysis, including financial statements, earnings reports, and industry research. Understand how to interpret and analyse these resources to make informed investment decisions.

Trading journals and tracking tools:
Consider using trading journals and tracking tools to record and analyse your trades. These tools help you track performance, identify patterns, and learn from both successful and unsuccessful trades.

Stock market trading can be a rewarding endeavour for wealth creation. By understanding the basics of the stock market, investing in stocks with a long-term perspective, implementing effective trading strategies, managing risk, and leveraging trading tools and resources, you can navigate the stock market with confidence.

Remember to continually educate yourself, stay disciplined, and adapt your trading approach based on market conditions and your own experiences.

CHAPTER NINE

BUILDING MULTIPLE STREAMS OF INCOME

9.1 Introduction to Multiple Streams of Income

Building multiple streams of income is a powerful wealth creation strategy that can provide financial stability, diversification, and increased earning potential. In this chapter, we will explore various methods and approaches to create multiple streams of income.

9.2 Types of Income Streams

There are several types of income streams that you can consider when building multiple sources of income. This section will cover:

Active income:
Active income is earned through direct participation in work or services, such as salaries, wages, or self-employment income. We will discuss ways to maximize active income and potentially increase your earning capacity.

Passive income:
Passive income is generated with minimal effort or ongoing involvement once the initial setup is done. This includes income from rental properties, dividend-paying stocks, peer-to-peer lending, or royalties from intellectual property. Learn how to identify passive income opportunities and create sustainable sources of passive income.

Portfolio income:
Portfolio income is earned through investments, such as interest, dividends, capital gains, or profits from trading securities. We will explore different investment options that can generate portfolio income and strategies for optimizing investment returns.

Side businesses and entrepreneurship:
Starting a side business or engaging in entrepreneurship can be an excellent way to generate additional income. Discover various business ideas, strategies for success, and tips for balancing multiple ventures.

Online income:
The internet has opened up numerous opportunities to earn income online. This includes freelancing, creating and selling digital products, affiliate marketing, e-commerce, and online

courses. Explore the potential of online income and how to leverage digital platforms effectively.

9.3 Assessing Income Opportunities

When building multiple streams of income, it's important to assess income opportunities to ensure they align with your goals and resources. This section will cover:

Market analysis:
Conduct market research to identify income opportunities in areas of high demand or emerging trends. Analyse consumer needs, competition, and potential profitability.

Skill assessment:
Evaluate your skills, knowledge, and expertise to identify income opportunities that align with your strengths. Consider acquiring new skills or enhancing existing ones to broaden your income potential.

Resource evaluation:
Assess your financial resources, time availability, and available networks when considering different income opportunities. Determine the level of investment required and the potential returns.

Risk assessment:
Evaluate the risks associated with each income opportunity, including market volatility, competition, and potential challenges. Develop strategies to manage and mitigate these risks.

9.4 Balancing and Managing Multiple Income Streams

Managing multiple income streams requires effective organization and time management. This section will discuss strategies for balancing and managing multiple income streams, including:

Prioritization:
Prioritize income streams based on their potential returns, time commitment required, and personal preferences. Allocate your time and resources accordingly to ensure maximum effectiveness.

Automation and delegation:
Explore ways to automate or delegate certain tasks to free up your time and energy. This can involve hiring virtual assistants, utilizing technology tools, or outsourcing certain aspects of your income-generating activities.

Systems and processes:
Develop systems and processes to streamline your income-generating activities. Create standard

operating procedures, set up efficient workflows, and leverage technology to optimize your operations.

Continuous learning and improvement:
Stay abreast of industry trends, market changes, and new income opportunities. Continuously invest in your education and skill development to stay competitive and adapt to evolving circumstances.

9.5 Financial Management and Wealth Preservation

As you build multiple income streams, it is crucial to manage your finances effectively and preserve your wealth. This section will cover:

Budgeting and financial planning:
Create a comprehensive budget and financial plan to track your income, expenses, and savings. Set financial goals and develop strategies to achieve them.

Tax planning:
Implement tax planning strategies to optimize your tax efficiency. Consult with tax professionals to ensure compliance and take advantage of available tax deductions and credits.

Emergency funds and insurance:
Build emergency funds to handle unexpected financial challenges. Additionally, consider appropriate insurance coverage to protect your assets, income streams, and overall financial well-being.

Asset allocation and diversification:
Diversify your investments across different asset classes to spread risk and enhance portfolio stability. Review and rebalance your investment portfolio periodically to align with your financial goals and risk tolerance.

Building multiple streams of income can provide financial security, flexibility, and the potential for significant wealth creation.

By understanding the different types of income streams, assessing income opportunities, managing your time and resources effectively, and implementing sound financial management strategies, you can create a robust and diversified income portfolio.

Remember to continually evaluate and optimize your income streams based on changing market conditions and personal circumstances.

CHAPTER TEN

WEALTH PRESERVATION AND LEGACY PLANNING

10.1 Introduction to Wealth Preservation

Building wealth is an important accomplishment, but equally important is the preservation of that wealth for future generations. In this chapter, we will explore strategies for wealth preservation and legacy planning to ensure your hard-earned assets are protected and passed down to your heirs.

10.2 Estate Planning

Estate planning is a crucial component of wealth preservation. This section will cover essential aspects of estate planning, including:

Will and trust:
Understand the importance of creating a will and establishing trusts to ensure your assets are distributed according to your wishes. Learn about different types of trusts and their benefits in estate planning.

Power of attorney and healthcare directives:

Explore the significance of appointing a power of attorney and establishing healthcare directives to make important financial and medical decisions on your behalf if you become incapacitated.

Beneficiary designations:
Review and update beneficiary designations on retirement accounts, life insurance policies, and other assets to ensure they align with your estate planning goals.

Minimizing estate taxes:
Familiarize yourself with estate tax laws and consider strategies to minimize estate taxes, such as gifting, charitable giving, and utilizing tax-efficient vehicles like family limited partnerships or irrevocable life insurance trusts.

10.3 Trusts and Asset Protection

Trusts can be valuable tools for both estate planning and asset protection. This section will discuss:

Revocable living trusts:
Understand how revocable living trusts can provide flexibility, privacy, and avoid probate. Learn about funding the trust and selecting a trustee.

Irrevocable trusts:
Explore irrevocable trusts, such as asset protection trusts and generation-skipping trusts. Understand how these trusts can shield assets from creditors and ensure the preservation of wealth for future generations.

Family limited partnerships (FLPs):
Learn about FLPs and how they can be used for asset protection, estate planning, and family wealth management. Understand the role of general partners and limited partners within an FLP.

Domestic and offshore asset protection:
Consider the benefits and limitations of domestic and offshore asset protection strategies. Understand the legal and tax implications associated with these structures.

10.4 Charitable Giving and Philanthropy

Incorporating charitable giving and philanthropy into your wealth preservation plan can provide both personal fulfilment and tax advantages. This section will cover:

Donor-advised funds:
Learn about donor-advised funds, which allow you to contribute to a charitable account and

recommend grants to charitable organizations over time. Understand the tax benefits associated with donor-advised funds.

Charitable foundations:
Explore the option of establishing a private charitable foundation to support causes you are passionate about. Understand the legal and operational requirements involved in managing a foundation.

Impact investing:
Consider impact investing, which involves making investments that generate both financial returns and positive social or environmental impact. Understand the different approaches and investment vehicles available in impact investing.

10.5 Wealth Education and Family Governance

Preserving wealth goes beyond financial structures; it involves educating future generations about responsible wealth management and instilling core values. This section will discuss:

Wealth education for heirs:
Develop a plan for educating your heirs about financial literacy, wealth management principles,

and the responsibilities associated with inheriting wealth.

Family governance:
Establish a family governance structure that outlines decision-making processes, communication protocols, and mechanisms for resolving conflicts. This helps ensure the long-term sustainability of family wealth and promotes harmony among family members.

Succession planning:
Plan for the smooth transition of wealth and leadership to the next generation. Identify successors, develop a succession plan, and communicate the plan to relevant stakeholders.

10.6 Regular Review and Professional Guidance

Wealth preservation and legacy planning require regular review and professional guidance. This section will cover:

Regular review:
Regularly review your estate plan, trust documents, and beneficiary designations to ensure they reflect your current wishes and circumstances. Update your plan as needed due

to changes in laws, family dynamics, or personal goals.

Professional advisors:
Seek the assistance of experienced professionals, such as estate planning attorneys, financial advisors, and tax experts, to guide you through the complexities of wealth preservation and legacy planning. They can help ensure your strategies are legally compliant and tailored to your specific needs.

Preserving wealth and planning for your legacy is a critical step in your financial journey. By implementing effective estate planning strategies, establishing trusts for asset protection, incorporating charitable giving and philanthropy, educating future generations, and seeking professional guidance, you can ensure the preservation and meaningful distribution of your wealth for generations to come.

Remember to regularly review and update your plans to adapt to changing circumstances and goals.

CHAPTER ELEVEN

MASTERING THE PSYCHOLOGY OF WEALTH

11.1 Introduction to the Psychology of Wealth

Achieving wealth is not just about financial strategies and investments; it also involves understanding and mastering the psychology of wealth. In this chapter, we will explore the mindset, attitudes, and behaviours that contribute to long-term financial success.

11.2 Developing a Wealth Mindset

A wealth mindset is the foundation for building and sustaining wealth. This section will cover key elements of developing a wealth mindset, including:

Abundance mindset:
Cultivate an abundance mindset that focuses on opportunities, growth, and possibilities rather than scarcity and limitations. Adopting a positive and optimistic outlook can attract wealth and open doors to new possibilities.

Self-belief and confidence:
Develop self-belief and confidence in your ability to create and manage wealth. Overcome limiting beliefs and self-doubt that may hinder your financial progress.

Goal setting and visualization:
Set clear and specific financial goals and create a vivid mental image of your desired financial future. Visualization techniques can help reinforce your goals and motivate you to take action.

Persistence and resilience:
Embrace persistence and resilience in the face of challenges and setbacks. Understand that building wealth takes time and effort, and setbacks are part of the journey. Learn from failures, adapt, and keep moving forward.

11.3 Overcoming Limiting Beliefs and Mindset Blocks

Many individuals hold limiting beliefs and mindset blocks that hinder their financial success. This section will discuss strategies for overcoming these obstacles, including:

Identifying limiting beliefs:
Identify and challenge your limiting beliefs about money, wealth, and success. Common limiting

beliefs include "money is the root of all evil" or "I'm not good with money." Replace these beliefs with empowering and positive beliefs that align with your financial goals.

Positive affirmations:
Use positive affirmations to reprogram your subconscious mind and reinforce empowering beliefs about money and wealth. Repeat affirmations daily to reinforce positive thought patterns.

Personal growth and self-improvement:
Invest in personal growth and self-improvement activities, such as reading books, attending seminars, or working with a coach or mentor. Continuous learning and personal development can help you overcome mindset blocks and expand your financial mindset.

11.4 Emotions and Money Management

Emotions play a significant role in financial decision-making. This section will explore how to manage emotions effectively when it comes to money, including:

Emotional awareness:
Cultivate self-awareness of your emotions and how they influence your financial decisions.

Recognize emotional triggers, such as fear, greed, or impulsivity, and develop strategies to manage them.

Rational decision-making:
Make financial decisions based on rational analysis and long-term goals rather than succumbing to short-term emotional impulses. Take time to evaluate the potential risks and rewards before making important financial choices.

Stress management:
Develop effective stress management techniques to avoid making impulsive or irrational financial decisions during stressful times. This may include practicing mindfulness, exercise, or seeking support from loved ones or professionals.

11.5 Building Healthy Financial Habits

Building healthy financial habits is crucial for long-term wealth creation. This section will discuss essential financial habits, including:

Budgeting and tracking expenses:
Create a budget to track your income and expenses. Understand where your money is going and identify areas where you can make adjustments to increase savings and investments.

Saving and investing:
Develop a habit of regular saving and disciplined investing. Automate savings and investment contributions to ensure consistent progress towards your financial goals.

Debt management:
Practice responsible debt management by minimizing high-interest debt and prioritizing debt repayment. Develop strategies to avoid unnecessary debt and leverage debt for wealth-building purposes when appropriate.

Continuous learning and financial literacy:
Commit to ongoing financial education and learning. Stay updated on financial trends, investment strategies, and personal finance best practices. The more knowledgeable you are, the better equipped you'll be to make informed financial decisions.

11.6 Cultivating Gratitude and Giving Back

Wealth creation is not just about personal gain; it is also an opportunity to give back and make a positive impact. This section will discuss:

Gratitude practice:
Cultivate a habit of gratitude by regularly expressing appreciation for the abundance in your

life. Recognize the progress you have made on your financial journey and appreciate the opportunities available to you.

Philanthropy and giving back:
Explore ways to give back to society and make a positive impact through charitable contributions, volunteering, or supporting causes you care about. Giving back not only benefits others but also brings a sense of fulfilment and purpose to your financial journey.

Mastering the psychology of wealth is a fundamental aspect of achieving long-term financial success.

By developing a wealth mindset, overcoming limiting beliefs, managing emotions, building healthy financial habits, and cultivating gratitude and generosity, you can create a solid foundation for sustainable wealth creation.

Remember, wealth is not just about money; it is about living a fulfilling and purposeful life while making a positive impact on the world around you.

CHAPTER TWELVE

CREATING A WEALTHY FUTURE

12.1 The Importance of Future Planning

Creating a wealthy future requires careful planning and foresight. In this chapter, we will explore the key elements of creating a wealthy future and securing your financial well-being.

12.2 Retirement Planning

Retirement planning is a critical aspect of creating a wealthy future. This section will cover essential considerations for retirement planning, including:

Setting retirement goals:
Define your retirement goals and envision the lifestyle you desire during your golden years. Consider factors such as desired retirement age, estimated expenses, and desired standard of living.

Retirement savings vehicles:
Explore different retirement savings vehicles, such as employer-sponsored retirement plans (e.g., 401(k), pension plans), individual retirement accounts (IRA), and annuities. Understand the

contribution limits, tax advantages, and investment options associated with each.

Investment strategies:
Develop investment strategies that align with your retirement goals and risk tolerance. Consider diversifying your portfolio, investing in a mix of stocks, bonds, and other assets, and periodically reviewing and adjusting your investment allocations.

Social Security and Medicare:
Understand the benefits and eligibility requirements of Social Security and Medicare. Familiarize yourself with the claiming strategies and options available to maximize your benefits.

12.3 Wealth Transfer and Succession Planning

Wealth transfer and succession planning ensure that your assets are transferred smoothly to the next generation. This section will cover important aspects of wealth transfer planning, including:

Estate planning and wills:
Review and update your estate plan and will to reflect your current wishes and ensure a smooth transition of assets. Consider working with estate

planning professionals to navigate complex legal and tax requirements.

Trusts and beneficiary designations:
Explore the use of trusts and beneficiary designations to facilitate the transfer of assets to your intended beneficiaries. Understand the different types of trusts and their benefits in wealth transfer and asset protection.

Family discussions and communication:
Initiate open and honest conversations with your family members about your wealth transfer plans. Clearly communicate your intentions, values, and expectations to foster understanding and minimize potential conflicts.

Business succession planning:
If you own a business, develop a comprehensive succession plan to ensure a smooth transition of ownership and management. Identify and groom potential successors, outline decision-making processes, and address key operational and legal considerations.

12.4 Continual Learning and Adaptation

To create a wealthy future, it's important to commit to continual learning and adaptation. This section will discuss strategies for ongoing growth and adaptation, including:

Financial education:
Continue to invest in your financial education by reading books, attending seminars, and staying informed about current financial trends and strategies. Embrace a growth mindset and seek opportunities to expand your knowledge and skills.

Monitoring and adjusting:
Regularly monitor your financial progress and make adjustments as needed. Review your investment portfolio, reassess your goals, and adapt your strategies based on changing market conditions or personal circumstances.

Seeking professional advice:
Consult with financial advisors, tax professionals, and legal experts to ensure your financial plans are aligned with your goals and optimize your financial strategies. Leverage their expertise to navigate complex financial matters.

12.4 Giving Back and Leaving a Legacy

Creating a wealthy future involves not only securing your own financial well-being but also leaving a positive legacy. This section will cover:

Philanthropy and charitable giving:
Incorporate philanthropy and charitable giving into your wealth creation plan. Identify causes and organizations that align with your values and contribute to making a positive impact on society.

Mentoring and supporting others:
Share your knowledge and expertise with others by mentoring aspiring entrepreneurs or individuals seeking financial guidance. Supporting others in their journey toward financial success can be personally rewarding and leave a lasting legacy.

Family values and traditions:
Define and articulate your family values and traditions to pass down to future generations. Create a framework for maintaining strong family bonds, instilling financial literacy, and promoting responsible wealth management.

Creating a wealthy future requires a combination of diligent planning, ongoing learning, adaptability, and a commitment to leaving a positive legacy.

By focusing on retirement planning, wealth transfer and succession planning, continual learning and adaptation, and giving back, you can set yourself up for a prosperous future while making a meaningful impact on the lives of others.

Remember to regularly review and adjust your plans as circumstances change, and seek professional guidance when needed.

CONCLUSION

Congratulations! You have reached the end of The Wealth Creation Handbook: Unlocking Financial Success. Throughout this book, we have explored various aspects of wealth creation, from developing a wealth mindset to setting financial goals, managing personal finances, investing, entrepreneurship, real estate, stock market trading, building multiple streams of income, wealth preservation and legacy planning, mastering the psychology of wealth, and creating a wealthy future.

We have learned that building wealth is not just about accumulating money; it's about adopting the right mindset, making informed decisions, and taking consistent action towards your financial goals. It requires discipline, perseverance, and a willingness to learn and adapt.

By cultivating a wealth mindset, setting clear financial goals, and managing your personal finances effectively, you have laid a solid foundation for wealth creation. Through various investment strategies and exploring different avenues such as entrepreneurship, real estate, stock market trading, and multiple streams of income, you have expanded your wealth-building potential.

We have also emphasized the importance of wealth preservation and legacy planning. By understanding estate planning, trusts, asset protection, and charitable giving, you have taken steps to secure your wealth for future generations and leave a lasting legacy.

Moreover, we have delved into the psychology of wealth and explored the significance of overcoming limiting beliefs, managing emotions, and building healthy financial habits. By mastering the psychological aspects of wealth, you are better equipped to make sound financial decisions and sustain long-term success.

Finally, we have highlighted the importance of creating a wealthy future through retirement planning, wealth transfer, ongoing learning, and giving back. By planning for your retirement, ensuring a smooth transfer of assets, continuously expanding your knowledge, and making a positive impact on society, you are creating a legacy that extends beyond monetary wealth.

Remember, wealth creation is a lifelong journey. It requires continuous learning, adaptation, and a commitment to personal growth. As you embark on your wealth creation journey, embrace challenges as opportunities, stay focused on your goals, and remain disciplined in your financial strategies.

Thank you for joining us on this journey to unlock financial success. We hope that The Wealth Creation Handbook has provided you with valuable insights, practical strategies, and inspiration to pursue your financial goals and create a life of abundance and prosperity. May you continue to thrive and make a positive impact in the world through your financial success.

APPENDIX: ADDITIONAL RESOURCES

1. Books on Wealth Creation:
- "Think and Grow Rich" by Napoleon Hill
- "The Millionaire Next Door" by Thomas J. Stanley and William D. Danko
- "Rich Dad Poor Dad" by Robert T. Kiyosaki
- "The Intelligent Investor" by Benjamin Graham
- "The Richest Man in Babylon" by George S. Clason

2. Websites and Blogs:
- Investopedia (www.investopedia.com)
- The Balance (www.thebalance.com)
- Financial Samurai (www.financialsamurai.com)
- BiggerPockets (www.biggerpockets.com)
- Mr. Money Mustache (www.mrmoneymustache.com)

3. Online Courses and Webinars:
- Coursera (www.coursera.org)
- Udemy (www.udemy.com)
- Khan Academy (www.khanacademy.org)
- Investopedia Academy (www.investopedia.com/academy)
- Financial Peace University (www.daveramsey.com/fpu)

4. Financial Tools and Apps:
- Mint: A budgeting app that helps track expenses and manage personal finances.

- Personal Capital: An investment and financial planning tool that provides a holistic view of your financial situation.
- Acorns: An app that automatically invests spare change from everyday purchases.
- Robinhood: A commission-free stock trading app for beginners and experienced investors.
- Zillow: A real estate app that provides information on properties, mortgages, and rental rates.

NOTES

NOTES

NOTES

www.ingramcontent.com/pod-product-compliance
Lightning Source LLC
Chambersburg PA
CBHW070121230526
45472CB00004B/1360